50 The Essential Baking Guide Recipes

By: Kelly Johnson

Table of Contents

- Classic French Baguette
- Chocolate Chip Cookies
- Sourdough Bread
- Lemon Pound Cake
- Apple Cinnamon Rolls
- Croissants
- Banana Bread
- Brioche Buns
- Red Velvet Cake
- Soft Pretzels
- Pumpkin Pie
- Cinnamon Swirl Bread
- Almond Croissants
- Blueberry Muffins
- Carrot Cake with Cream Cheese Frosting
- Rustic Focaccia
- Cherry Clafoutis
- Chocolate Eclairs
- Brioche French Toast
- Madeleines
- Vanilla Cupcakes
- Pecan Pie
- Chocolate Lava Cake
- Raspberry Tart
- Lemon Meringue Pie
- Poppy Seed Bread
- Rye Bread
- Oatmeal Cookies
- Chocolate Truffles
- Swiss Roll
- Sticky Buns
- Coconut Macaroons
- Strawberry Shortcake
- Walnut Banana Bread
- Peach Galette

- Tiramisu
- Zucchini Bread
- Classic Cheesecake
- Raspberry Almond Bars
- Apricot Danish
- Cardamom Bread
- Fig and Walnut Bread
- Key Lime Pie
- Pumpkin Spice Cake
- Chocolate Hazelnut Tart
- Pear and Almond Cake
- Nutella Swirl Bread
- Honey and Lavender Madeleines
- Salted Caramel Brownies
- Sweet Potato Pie

Classic French Baguette

Ingredients:

- 3 1/2 cups all-purpose flour
- 1 1/2 tsp salt
- 1 tsp sugar
- 1 packet (2 1/4 tsp) active dry yeast
- 1 1/4 cups warm water (110°F)
- 1 tbsp olive oil

Instructions:

1. In a bowl, dissolve the sugar and yeast in warm water. Let sit for 5-10 minutes until frothy.
2. In a large bowl, mix flour and salt. Add the yeast mixture and olive oil. Stir to form a dough.
3. Knead the dough for 8-10 minutes until smooth and elastic. Place in a lightly oiled bowl, cover, and let rise for 1-2 hours or until doubled in size.
4. Punch the dough down and divide it into two equal portions. Shape each into a long baguette shape.
5. Place the shaped dough on a baking sheet lined with parchment paper. Let rise for 30-60 minutes.
6. Preheat the oven to 475°F (245°C). Make a few slashes on top of each baguette with a sharp knife.
7. Bake for 20-25 minutes until golden brown. Cool before serving.

Chocolate Chip Cookies

Ingredients:

- 1 cup (2 sticks) unsalted butter, softened
- 3/4 cup white sugar
- 3/4 cup packed brown sugar
- 2 tsp vanilla extract
- 2 large eggs
- 2 1/4 cups all-purpose flour
- 1 tsp baking soda
- 1/2 tsp salt
- 2 cups semisweet chocolate chips

Instructions:

1. Preheat the oven to 350°F (175°C). Line baking sheets with parchment paper.
2. In a large bowl, cream together the butter, white sugar, and brown sugar until smooth.
3. Add vanilla extract and eggs, one at a time, beating well after each addition.
4. In a separate bowl, combine flour, baking soda, and salt. Gradually add to the butter mixture and stir until well combined.
5. Fold in the chocolate chips.
6. Drop spoonfuls of dough onto the prepared baking sheets, spaced about 2 inches apart.
7. Bake for 10-12 minutes until the edges are golden. Cool on wire racks.

Sourdough Bread

Ingredients:

- 1 cup sourdough starter (active and bubbly)
- 1 1/2 cups warm water
- 4 cups all-purpose flour
- 2 tsp salt

Instructions:

1. In a large mixing bowl, combine the sourdough starter and warm water. Stir in the flour and salt to form a sticky dough.
2. Knead the dough for 8-10 minutes until smooth and elastic. Place the dough in a lightly oiled bowl, cover, and let rise for 4-6 hours or overnight.
3. Punch down the dough and shape it into a round loaf. Place on a baking sheet lined with parchment paper.
4. Preheat the oven to 450°F (230°C). Let the dough rise for another 1-2 hours.
5. Use a sharp knife to score the top of the dough. Bake for 30-40 minutes until the crust is golden and the bread sounds hollow when tapped on the bottom.
6. Let cool before slicing.

Lemon Pound Cake

Ingredients:

- 1 1/2 cups all-purpose flour
- 1 tsp baking powder
- 1/4 tsp salt
- 1 cup unsalted butter, softened
- 1 1/2 cups granulated sugar
- 4 large eggs
- 1 tbsp lemon zest
- 1/4 cup fresh lemon juice
- 1 tsp vanilla extract
- 1/2 cup sour cream

Instructions:

1. Preheat the oven to 350°F (175°C). Grease and flour a loaf pan.
2. In a medium bowl, whisk together the flour, baking powder, and salt.
3. In a large bowl, beat the butter and sugar until light and fluffy. Add the eggs, one at a time, beating well after each addition.
4. Stir in lemon zest, lemon juice, and vanilla extract.
5. Gradually add the dry ingredients, alternating with the sour cream, until just combined.
6. Pour the batter into the prepared loaf pan and smooth the top.
7. Bake for 55-60 minutes, or until a toothpick inserted into the center comes out clean. Let cool in the pan for 10 minutes, then transfer to a wire rack to cool completely.

Apple Cinnamon Rolls

Ingredients:

- 1 cup warm milk
- 2 tsp active dry yeast
- 1/2 cup granulated sugar
- 4 cups all-purpose flour
- 1/2 tsp salt
- 1/4 cup unsalted butter, softened
- 2 large eggs
- 2 apples, peeled and chopped
- 2 tbsp cinnamon
- 1/2 cup brown sugar

Instructions:

1. In a small bowl, dissolve yeast and sugar in warm milk. Let sit for 5-10 minutes until frothy.
2. In a large bowl, combine flour and salt. Add yeast mixture, butter, and eggs. Stir to form a dough, then knead for 8-10 minutes.
3. Place the dough in a lightly oiled bowl, cover, and let rise for 1 hour.
4. Punch down the dough and roll it out into a rectangle.
5. Spread cinnamon and brown sugar evenly over the dough. Sprinkle chopped apples over the cinnamon sugar mixture.
6. Roll the dough up tightly and slice into 12 rolls.
7. Place the rolls on a greased baking dish, cover, and let rise for 30 minutes.
8. Preheat the oven to 350°F (175°C). Bake for 20-25 minutes until golden brown. Serve warm.

Croissants

Ingredients:

- 1 1/2 cups all-purpose flour
- 1/2 cup cold unsalted butter, cut into small pieces
- 1/2 cup warm milk
- 2 tbsp sugar
- 1 tsp salt
- 1 tbsp instant yeast
- 1 egg, beaten (for egg wash)

Instructions:

1. In a large mixing bowl, combine flour, sugar, and salt. Add the butter and rub it in until the mixture resembles coarse crumbs.
2. Dissolve yeast in warm milk and add it to the flour mixture. Mix to form a dough.
3. Knead the dough on a floured surface for 5-7 minutes. Cover and refrigerate for 1 hour.
4. Roll out the dough into a rectangle. Fold the dough into thirds like a letter and refrigerate for 30 minutes.
5. Repeat the folding process two more times, chilling between folds.
6. Roll out the dough into a long rectangle, then cut into triangles. Roll each triangle into a croissant shape.
7. Place the croissants on a baking sheet, brush with egg wash, and let rise for 1 hour.
8. Preheat the oven to 375°F (190°C). Bake for 15-20 minutes, until golden brown. Cool before serving.

Banana Bread

Ingredients:

- 2 ripe bananas, mashed
- 1/2 cup unsalted butter, melted
- 1 cup granulated sugar
- 2 eggs
- 1 tsp vanilla extract
- 1 1/2 cups all-purpose flour
- 1 tsp baking powder
- 1/2 tsp baking soda
- 1/2 tsp salt

Instructions:

1. Preheat the oven to 350°F (175°C). Grease a loaf pan.
2. In a large bowl, mix mashed bananas, melted butter, sugar, eggs, and vanilla.
3. In a separate bowl, whisk together flour, baking powder, baking soda, and salt. Gradually add to the banana mixture.
4. Pour the batter into the prepared loaf pan and smooth the top.
5. Bake for 50-60 minutes, or until a toothpick inserted into the center comes out clean. Let cool before slicing.

Brioche Buns

Ingredients:

- 1/2 cup warm milk
- 2 tsp active dry yeast
- 1/4 cup granulated sugar
- 3 1/2 cups all-purpose flour
- 1 tsp salt
- 4 large eggs
- 1/2 cup unsalted butter, softened
- 1 egg (for egg wash)

Instructions:

1. In a small bowl, dissolve yeast and sugar in warm milk. Let sit for 5-10 minutes until frothy.
2. In a large bowl, combine flour and salt. Add yeast mixture and eggs, mixing to form a dough.
3. Knead the dough for 8-10 minutes, then add butter a little at a time, kneading until incorporated.
4. Cover the dough and let rise for 1-2 hours or until doubled in size.
5. Punch down the dough and divide it into 8 equal portions. Shape each portion into a bun and place on a greased baking sheet.
6. Let the buns rise for 1 hour.
7. Preheat the oven to 375°F (190°C). Brush the buns with egg wash.
8. Bake for 15-18 minutes, until golden brown. Cool before serving.

Red Velvet Cake

Ingredients:

- 2 1/2 cups all-purpose flour
- 1 1/2 cups granulated sugar
- 1 tsp baking powder
- 1 tsp baking soda
- 1 tsp cocoa powder
- 1/2 tsp salt
- 1 cup buttermilk, room temperature
- 1/2 cup unsalted butter, softened
- 2 large eggs
- 1 tbsp red food coloring
- 1 tsp vanilla extract
- 1 tsp white vinegar

Cream Cheese Frosting:

- 8 oz cream cheese, softened
- 1/2 cup unsalted butter, softened
- 4 cups powdered sugar
- 1 tsp vanilla extract

Instructions:

1. Preheat the oven to 350°F (175°C) and grease two 9-inch round cake pans.
2. In a large bowl, whisk together the flour, sugar, baking powder, baking soda, cocoa powder, and salt.
3. In a separate bowl, beat together the buttermilk, butter, eggs, red food coloring, and vanilla extract.
4. Add the wet ingredients to the dry ingredients and mix until smooth. Stir in the vinegar.
5. Divide the batter evenly between the prepared cake pans and bake for 25-30 minutes, or until a toothpick comes out clean.
6. Let the cakes cool in the pans for 10 minutes, then transfer to a wire rack to cool completely.
7. For the frosting, beat the cream cheese and butter together until creamy. Gradually add the powdered sugar and vanilla, and beat until smooth.
8. Frost the cooled cakes with the cream cheese frosting and serve.

Soft Pretzels

Ingredients:

- 1 1/2 cups warm water
- 1 tbsp sugar
- 2 1/4 tsp active dry yeast
- 4 cups all-purpose flour
- 1 tsp salt
- 2 tbsp unsalted butter, melted
- 10 cups water
- 2/3 cup baking soda
- Coarse salt for sprinkling

Instructions:

1. In a small bowl, dissolve the sugar and yeast in warm water. Let sit for 5 minutes until frothy.
2. In a large bowl, combine the flour, salt, and melted butter. Add the yeast mixture and stir until a dough forms.
3. Knead the dough on a floured surface for 5-7 minutes, then cover and let rise for 1 hour, or until doubled in size.
4. Preheat the oven to 425°F (220°C) and line a baking sheet with parchment paper.
5. In a large pot, bring 10 cups of water to a boil and stir in the baking soda.
6. Punch down the dough and divide it into 8 equal portions. Roll each portion into a long rope and shape into a pretzel.
7. Boil each pretzel for 30 seconds, then transfer to the baking sheet.
8. Sprinkle with coarse salt and bake for 12-15 minutes, until golden brown. Let cool before serving.

Pumpkin Pie

Ingredients:

- 1 pie crust (store-bought or homemade)
- 2 cups pumpkin puree
- 1 cup heavy cream
- 3/4 cup granulated sugar
- 1/2 tsp ground cinnamon
- 1/4 tsp ground ginger
- 1/4 tsp ground nutmeg
- 1/4 tsp salt
- 2 large eggs
- 1 tsp vanilla extract

Instructions:

1. Preheat the oven to 425°F (220°C).
2. In a large bowl, whisk together the pumpkin puree, heavy cream, sugar, spices, and salt.
3. Beat in the eggs and vanilla extract until smooth.
4. Pour the pumpkin mixture into the pie crust.
5. Bake for 15 minutes, then reduce the temperature to 350°F (175°C) and bake for an additional 40-45 minutes, until the filling is set.
6. Cool completely before slicing and serving.

Cinnamon Swirl Bread

Ingredients:

- 2 1/4 cups all-purpose flour
- 1 packet active dry yeast
- 1/2 cup warm milk
- 1/4 cup granulated sugar
- 1/2 tsp salt
- 1/4 cup unsalted butter, softened
- 2 large eggs
- 1/4 cup brown sugar
- 1 tbsp ground cinnamon

Instructions:

1. In a small bowl, dissolve the sugar and yeast in warm milk. Let sit for 5 minutes until frothy.
2. In a large bowl, combine the flour and salt. Add the yeast mixture, butter, and eggs. Stir until a dough forms.
3. Knead the dough for 5-7 minutes, then cover and let rise for 1 hour.
4. Preheat the oven to 350°F (175°C) and grease a loaf pan.
5. Punch down the dough and roll it out into a rectangle.
6. Sprinkle the brown sugar and cinnamon over the dough. Roll it up tightly and place in the loaf pan.
7. Let rise for 30 minutes, then bake for 30-35 minutes, until golden brown.
8. Cool in the pan for 10 minutes, then transfer to a wire rack.

Almond Croissants

Ingredients:

- 4 croissants (preferably day-old)
- 1/2 cup almond paste
- 1/4 cup powdered sugar
- 1/4 cup unsalted butter, softened
- 1 egg, beaten (for egg wash)
- Sliced almonds for topping

Instructions:

1. Preheat the oven to 350°F (175°C).
2. Slice the croissants in half lengthwise and place on a baking sheet.
3. In a small bowl, mix together the almond paste, powdered sugar, and softened butter.
4. Spread the almond mixture evenly inside each croissant.
5. Brush the tops of the croissants with the beaten egg and sprinkle with sliced almonds.
6. Bake for 10-12 minutes, until golden brown and slightly crispy. Serve warm.

Blueberry Muffins

Ingredients:

- 1 1/2 cups all-purpose flour
- 3/4 cup granulated sugar
- 2 tsp baking powder
- 1/2 tsp baking soda
- 1/4 tsp salt
- 1/2 cup unsalted butter, melted
- 2 large eggs
- 1/2 cup buttermilk
- 1 tsp vanilla extract
- 1 1/2 cups fresh blueberries

Instructions:

1. Preheat the oven to 350°F (175°C) and line a muffin tin with paper liners.
2. In a large bowl, whisk together the flour, sugar, baking powder, baking soda, and salt.
3. In a separate bowl, whisk together the melted butter, eggs, buttermilk, and vanilla extract.
4. Pour the wet ingredients into the dry ingredients and stir until just combined.
5. Gently fold in the blueberries.
6. Divide the batter evenly among the muffin cups.
7. Bake for 18-20 minutes, or until a toothpick comes out clean. Cool in the pan for 5 minutes, then transfer to a wire rack.

Carrot Cake with Cream Cheese Frosting

Ingredients:

- 2 cups all-purpose flour
- 2 tsp baking powder
- 1/2 tsp baking soda
- 1/2 tsp ground cinnamon
- 1/4 tsp ground nutmeg
- 1/2 tsp salt
- 1 1/2 cups granulated sugar
- 1 cup vegetable oil
- 4 large eggs
- 2 tsp vanilla extract
- 2 cups grated carrots
- 1/2 cup chopped walnuts (optional)

Cream Cheese Frosting:

- 8 oz cream cheese, softened
- 1/2 cup unsalted butter, softened
- 4 cups powdered sugar
- 1 tsp vanilla extract

Instructions:

1. Preheat the oven to 350°F (175°C) and grease two 9-inch round cake pans.
2. In a large bowl, whisk together the flour, baking powder, baking soda, cinnamon, nutmeg, and salt.
3. In a separate bowl, beat together the sugar, oil, eggs, and vanilla extract.
4. Gradually add the dry ingredients to the wet mixture and stir until just combined.
5. Stir in the grated carrots and walnuts (if using).
6. Pour the batter into the prepared cake pans and bake for 30-35 minutes, until a toothpick comes out clean.
7. For the frosting, beat the cream cheese and butter together until creamy. Gradually add the powdered sugar and vanilla, and beat until smooth.
8. Frost the cooled cakes with the cream cheese frosting and serve.

Rustic Focaccia

Ingredients:

- 2 cups all-purpose flour
- 1 packet active dry yeast
- 1 cup warm water
- 2 tbsp olive oil
- 1 tsp salt
- Fresh rosemary leaves
- Coarse sea salt

Instructions:

1. In a small bowl, dissolve the yeast in warm water. Let sit for 5 minutes until frothy.
2. In a large bowl, combine the flour and salt. Add the yeast mixture and olive oil, and stir until a dough forms.
3. Knead the dough for 5-7 minutes, then cover and let rise for 1 hour, or until doubled in size.
4. Preheat the oven to 400°F (200°C).
5. Punch down the dough and transfer to a greased baking sheet. Use your fingers to spread the dough out.
6. Drizzle with olive oil and sprinkle with rosemary and sea salt.
7. Bake for 20-25 minutes, until golden brown. Let cool before serving.

Cherry Clafoutis

Ingredients:

- 2 cups fresh cherries, pitted
- 3/4 cup whole milk
- 1/4 cup heavy cream
- 1/2 cup granulated sugar
- 3 large eggs
- 1 tsp vanilla extract
- 1/4 tsp salt
- 1/2 cup all-purpose flour
- Powdered sugar for dusting

Instructions:

1. Preheat the oven to 375°F (190°C) and grease a 9-inch round baking dish.
2. Arrange the cherries evenly in the bottom of the dish.
3. In a mixing bowl, whisk together the milk, heavy cream, sugar, eggs, vanilla extract, and salt.
4. Gradually add the flour and mix until smooth.
5. Pour the batter over the cherries and bake for 35-40 minutes, or until the clafoutis is puffed and golden brown.
6. Let cool slightly, then dust with powdered sugar before serving.

Chocolate Eclairs

Ingredients:

- **For the choux pastry:**
    - 1 cup water
    - 1/2 cup unsalted butter
    - 1 cup all-purpose flour
    - 1/4 tsp salt
    - 4 large eggs
- **For the chocolate glaze:**
    - 4 oz semi-sweet chocolate
    - 1/4 cup heavy cream
- **For the filling:**
    - 1 cup heavy cream
    - 2 tbsp powdered sugar
    - 1 tsp vanilla extract

Instructions:

1. Preheat the oven to 425°F (220°C) and line a baking sheet with parchment paper.
2. In a saucepan, bring the water and butter to a boil. Add the flour and salt, stirring until the mixture forms a ball.
3. Remove from heat and add eggs one at a time, beating well after each addition.
4. Pipe the dough onto the baking sheet into 4-inch long logs.
5. Bake for 20-25 minutes, until golden and puffed. Let cool completely.
6. For the filling, whip the heavy cream, powdered sugar, and vanilla extract until stiff peaks form. Fill the eclairs with the whipped cream.
7. For the glaze, melt the chocolate and heavy cream together. Dip the tops of the eclairs into the glaze and let set.

Brioche French Toast

Ingredients:

- 4 slices of brioche bread
- 2 large eggs
- 1/2 cup milk
- 1/2 tsp cinnamon
- 1/4 tsp vanilla extract
- 1 tbsp butter
- Maple syrup for serving

Instructions:

1. In a bowl, whisk together the eggs, milk, cinnamon, and vanilla extract.
2. Heat a griddle or skillet over medium heat and melt the butter.
3. Dip each slice of brioche bread into the egg mixture, coating both sides.
4. Cook the bread on the griddle for 2-3 minutes per side, until golden brown.
5. Serve with maple syrup.

Madeleines

Ingredients:

- 1 cup all-purpose flour
- 1/2 cup unsalted butter, melted
- 1/2 cup granulated sugar
- 3 large eggs
- 1 tsp vanilla extract
- 1 tsp lemon zest
- 1/2 tsp baking powder
- Powdered sugar for dusting

Instructions:

1. Preheat the oven to 350°F (175°C) and grease a madeleine pan.
2. In a bowl, whisk together the flour, sugar, eggs, vanilla extract, lemon zest, and baking powder until smooth.
3. Fold in the melted butter until combined.
4. Spoon the batter into the madeleine pan, filling each mold about 3/4 full.
5. Bake for 10-12 minutes, until golden brown.
6. Let cool slightly, then dust with powdered sugar before serving.

Vanilla Cupcakes

Ingredients:

- 1 1/2 cups all-purpose flour
- 1 cup granulated sugar
- 1/2 tsp baking powder
- 1/4 tsp baking soda
- 1/4 tsp salt
- 1/2 cup unsalted butter, softened
- 2 large eggs
- 1 tsp vanilla extract
- 1/2 cup milk

Vanilla Frosting:

- 1/2 cup unsalted butter, softened
- 2 cups powdered sugar
- 1 tsp vanilla extract
- 2-3 tbsp milk

Instructions:

1. Preheat the oven to 350°F (175°C) and line a muffin tin with paper liners.
2. In a bowl, whisk together the flour, sugar, baking powder, baking soda, and salt.
3. In a separate bowl, beat the butter, eggs, and vanilla extract until smooth.
4. Gradually add the dry ingredients, alternating with the milk, mixing until combined.
5. Spoon the batter into the cupcake liners, filling each about 2/3 full.
6. Bake for 18-20 minutes, or until a toothpick comes out clean. Let cool completely.
7. For the frosting, beat the butter and powdered sugar together until smooth. Add the vanilla extract and milk, and beat until creamy.
8. Frost the cooled cupcakes and serve.

Pecan Pie

Ingredients:

- 1 pie crust (store-bought or homemade)
- 1 cup corn syrup
- 1 cup granulated sugar
- 1/4 cup unsalted butter, melted
- 3 large eggs
- 1 1/2 cups pecans, chopped
- 1 tsp vanilla extract
- 1/4 tsp salt

Instructions:

1. Preheat the oven to 350°F (175°C) and place the pie crust in a pie dish.
2. In a bowl, whisk together the corn syrup, sugar, butter, eggs, vanilla extract, and salt.
3. Stir in the pecans and pour the mixture into the pie crust.
4. Bake for 50-60 minutes, until the filling is set and golden brown.
5. Let cool completely before serving.

Chocolate Lava Cake

Ingredients:

- 1/2 cup unsalted butter
- 6 oz semi-sweet chocolate
- 1 cup powdered sugar
- 2 large eggs
- 2 large egg yolks
- 1/4 tsp vanilla extract
- 1/4 cup all-purpose flour
- Pinch of salt

Instructions:

1. Preheat the oven to 425°F (220°C) and grease 4 ramekins.
2. In a microwave-safe bowl, melt the butter and chocolate together, stirring until smooth.
3. Whisk in the powdered sugar, eggs, egg yolks, and vanilla extract until well combined.
4. Stir in the flour and salt.
5. Divide the batter evenly among the ramekins and bake for 12-14 minutes, until the edges are set and the center is soft.
6. Let cool for 1 minute, then invert onto plates. Serve warm with ice cream.

Raspberry Tart

Ingredients:

- 1 tart crust (store-bought or homemade)
- 1/2 cup heavy cream
- 8 oz cream cheese, softened
- 1/4 cup powdered sugar
- 1 tsp vanilla extract
- 1 pint fresh raspberries
- 1/4 cup apricot jam, melted

Instructions:

1. Preheat the oven to 350°F (175°C) and bake the tart crust according to package directions or until golden brown.
2. In a bowl, beat the heavy cream, cream cheese, powdered sugar, and vanilla extract until smooth.
3. Spread the cream mixture evenly into the cooled tart crust.
4. Arrange the raspberries on top in a circular pattern.
5. Brush the melted apricot jam over the raspberries to glaze them.
6. Refrigerate for at least 2 hours before serving.

Lemon Meringue Pie

Ingredients:

- **For the crust:**
    - 1 1/4 cups all-purpose flour
    - 1/4 tsp salt
    - 1/2 cup unsalted butter, cold and cubed
    - 3-4 tbsp ice water
- **For the filling:**
    - 1 cup granulated sugar
    - 2 tbsp cornstarch
    - 1/4 tsp salt
    - 1 1/2 cups water
    - 3 large egg yolks, beaten
    - 2 tbsp unsalted butter
    - 1/2 cup fresh lemon juice
    - 1 tbsp lemon zest
    - 1/2 tsp vanilla extract
- **For the meringue:**
    - 3 large egg whites
    - 1/4 tsp cream of tartar
    - 1/2 cup granulated sugar

Instructions:

1. **For the crust:** Preheat the oven to 425°F (220°C). In a food processor, pulse the flour and salt. Add the butter and pulse until the mixture resembles coarse crumbs. Gradually add ice water and pulse until the dough comes together. Roll out the dough and fit it into a 9-inch pie dish. Bake for 12-15 minutes, or until golden brown. Let cool.
2. **For the filling:** In a saucepan, whisk together sugar, cornstarch, and salt. Gradually add water, then cook over medium heat, stirring constantly, until thickened. Whisk a little of the hot mixture into the egg yolks, then slowly whisk the egg yolk mixture back into the saucepan. Cook for another 2 minutes. Remove from heat, and stir in butter, lemon juice, lemon zest, and vanilla.
3. **For the meringue:** Beat egg whites and cream of tartar until soft peaks form. Gradually add sugar and continue beating until stiff peaks form. Spread the meringue over the pie, sealing the edges.

4. Bake the pie at 350°F (175°C) for 10-12 minutes, until the meringue is golden brown. Let cool before serving.

Poppy Seed Bread

Ingredients:

- 1 1/2 cups all-purpose flour
- 1 tsp baking powder
- 1/2 tsp baking soda
- 1/4 tsp salt
- 1/4 cup poppy seeds
- 1/2 cup unsalted butter, softened
- 1 cup granulated sugar
- 2 large eggs
- 1 tsp vanilla extract
- 1 cup sour cream

Instructions:

1. Preheat the oven to 350°F (175°C) and grease a loaf pan.
2. In a bowl, whisk together the flour, baking powder, baking soda, salt, and poppy seeds.
3. In another bowl, cream the butter and sugar until light and fluffy. Add the eggs one at a time, beating well after each addition. Stir in the vanilla extract.
4. Add the dry ingredients alternately with the sour cream, beginning and ending with the dry ingredients. Mix until just combined.
5. Pour the batter into the prepared loaf pan and bake for 50-60 minutes, or until a toothpick inserted into the center comes out clean.
6. Let cool in the pan for 10 minutes before transferring to a wire rack to cool completely.

Rye Bread

Ingredients:

- 2 1/2 cups rye flour
- 1 1/2 cups all-purpose flour
- 2 tsp salt
- 1 tbsp sugar
- 1 tsp active dry yeast
- 1 1/4 cups warm water
- 1 tbsp olive oil
- 1 tbsp caraway seeds (optional)

Instructions:

1. In a large bowl, combine the rye flour, all-purpose flour, salt, and sugar. In a separate small bowl, dissolve the yeast in warm water and let sit for 5-10 minutes, until foamy.
2. Add the yeast mixture and olive oil to the dry ingredients. Mix until a dough forms.
3. Knead the dough on a floured surface for 8-10 minutes, until smooth. Place the dough in an oiled bowl, cover, and let rise for 1-2 hours, or until doubled in size.
4. Punch down the dough and shape it into a loaf. Place in a greased loaf pan and cover. Let rise for another 30-45 minutes.
5. Preheat the oven to 375°F (190°C). If desired, sprinkle caraway seeds on top of the dough. Bake for 35-40 minutes, or until the bread sounds hollow when tapped.
6. Let cool before slicing.

Oatmeal Cookies

Ingredients:

- 1 cup unsalted butter, softened
- 1 cup granulated sugar
- 1 cup packed brown sugar
- 2 large eggs
- 1 tsp vanilla extract
- 1 1/2 cups all-purpose flour
- 1 tsp baking soda
- 1/2 tsp cinnamon
- 1/4 tsp salt
- 3 cups rolled oats
- 1 cup raisins (optional)

Instructions:

1. Preheat the oven to 350°F (175°C) and line a baking sheet with parchment paper.
2. In a bowl, cream together the butter, granulated sugar, and brown sugar until light and fluffy. Add the eggs and vanilla extract, and mix well.
3. In another bowl, whisk together the flour, baking soda, cinnamon, and salt. Gradually add the dry ingredients to the wet ingredients and mix until combined.
4. Stir in the oats and raisins (if using).
5. Drop spoonfuls of dough onto the prepared baking sheet and bake for 10-12 minutes, until golden brown around the edges.
6. Let cool on a wire rack.

Chocolate Truffles

Ingredients:

- 8 oz semi-sweet chocolate, chopped
- 1/2 cup heavy cream
- 1 tsp vanilla extract
- Cocoa powder, powdered sugar, or chopped nuts for coating

Instructions:

1. Heat the cream in a saucepan until it just begins to simmer. Remove from heat and pour over the chopped chocolate. Let sit for 5 minutes.
2. Stir the chocolate and cream together until smooth and glossy. Stir in the vanilla extract.
3. Let the mixture cool to room temperature, then refrigerate for 1-2 hours, until firm.
4. Once firm, scoop out small portions of the mixture and roll into balls.
5. Roll the truffles in cocoa powder, powdered sugar, or chopped nuts to coat. Store in the refrigerator until ready to serve.

Swiss Roll

Ingredients:

- **For the cake:**
    - 3 large eggs
    - 3/4 cup granulated sugar
    - 1 tsp vanilla extract
    - 1/2 cup all-purpose flour
    - 1 tsp baking powder
    - 1/4 tsp salt
    - Powdered sugar for dusting
- **For the filling:**
    - 1 cup heavy cream
    - 1 tbsp powdered sugar
    - 1 tsp vanilla extract

Instructions:

1. Preheat the oven to 350°F (175°C) and line a 10x15-inch jelly roll pan with parchment paper.
2. Beat the eggs and sugar together until light and fluffy. Stir in the vanilla extract.
3. In a separate bowl, whisk together the flour, baking powder, and salt. Gradually fold the dry ingredients into the egg mixture.
4. Pour the batter into the prepared pan and smooth the top. Bake for 10-12 minutes, or until the cake springs back when lightly pressed.
5. Immediately remove the cake from the pan and roll it up in a clean kitchen towel dusted with powdered sugar. Let cool completely.
6. For the filling, whip the cream, powdered sugar, and vanilla extract until stiff peaks form.
7. Unroll the cooled cake, spread with the whipped cream, and roll it back up. Dust with powdered sugar before serving.

Sticky Buns

Ingredients:

- **For the dough:**
    - 1 cup warm milk
    - 1/4 cup granulated sugar
    - 2 tsp active dry yeast
    - 1/4 cup unsalted butter, melted
    - 1 tsp salt
    - 3 1/2 cups all-purpose flour
    - 1 large egg
- **For the filling:**
    - 1/2 cup unsalted butter, softened
    - 1 cup brown sugar, packed
    - 1 tbsp ground cinnamon
    - 1/2 cup chopped pecans or walnuts (optional)
- **For the sticky topping:**
    - 1/2 cup unsalted butter, melted
    - 1/2 cup brown sugar
    - 1/4 cup heavy cream
    - 1/2 tsp vanilla extract

Instructions:

1. In a bowl, combine warm milk, sugar, and yeast. Let sit for 5 minutes. Add the butter, salt, flour, and egg, and mix until a dough forms. Knead for 8-10 minutes, then let rise for 1 hour.
2. Roll out the dough into a rectangle and spread with softened butter. Sprinkle with brown sugar, cinnamon, and chopped nuts.
3. Roll up the dough tightly and slice into 12 pieces. Place the pieces in a greased baking dish.
4. Preheat the oven to 350°F (175°C) and bake for 25-30 minutes.
5. For the topping, combine melted butter, brown sugar, heavy cream, and vanilla extract. Pour over the warm buns and let soak before serving.

Coconut Macaroons

Ingredients:

- 2 1/2 cups sweetened shredded coconut
- 1/2 cup sweetened condensed milk
- 1/4 tsp vanilla extract
- 2 large egg whites
- 1/4 tsp salt

Instructions:

1. Preheat the oven to 325°F (165°C) and line a baking sheet with parchment paper.
2. In a bowl, mix together coconut, condensed milk, and vanilla extract.
3. In a separate bowl, beat the egg whites and salt until stiff peaks form.
4. Fold the egg whites into the coconut mixture until well combined.
5. Drop spoonfuls of the mixture onto the prepared baking sheet. Bake for 15-20 minutes, or until golden brown.
6. Let cool on a wire rack.

Strawberry Shortcake

Ingredients:

- **For the biscuits:**
    - 2 cups all-purpose flour
    - 2 tsp baking powder
    - 1/4 tsp salt
    - 2 tbsp granulated sugar
    - 1/2 cup unsalted butter, cold and cubed
    - 3/4 cup heavy cream
- **For the filling:**
    - 4 cups fresh strawberries, hulled and sliced
    - 1/4 cup granulated sugar
    - 1 tsp vanilla extract
- **For the whipped cream:**
    - 1 cup heavy cream
    - 2 tbsp powdered sugar
    - 1 tsp vanilla extract

Instructions:

1. **For the biscuits:** Preheat the oven to 425°F (220°C). In a large bowl, combine the flour, baking powder, salt, and sugar. Cut in the butter until the mixture resembles coarse crumbs. Gradually add the cream and stir until a dough forms. Pat the dough out onto a floured surface and cut into 8 rounds. Place on a baking sheet and bake for 12-15 minutes, or until golden brown. Let cool slightly.
2. **For the filling:** In a bowl, toss the strawberries with sugar and vanilla extract. Let sit for 10-15 minutes to macerate.
3. **For the whipped cream:** Beat the cream, powdered sugar, and vanilla extract until stiff peaks form.
4. To assemble, split the biscuits in half. Top the bottom half with the strawberry mixture and whipped cream. Place the top half of the biscuit on top and serve.

Walnut Banana Bread

Ingredients:

- 2 ripe bananas, mashed
- 1/3 cup unsalted butter, melted
- 1 tsp vanilla extract
- 1/2 cup brown sugar, packed
- 1 egg, beaten
- 1 tsp baking soda
- 1/4 tsp salt
- 1 1/2 cups all-purpose flour
- 1/2 cup chopped walnuts

Instructions:

1. Preheat the oven to 350°F (175°C) and grease a loaf pan.
2. In a bowl, mix together the mashed bananas, melted butter, vanilla extract, and brown sugar. Add the egg and mix well.
3. In a separate bowl, whisk together the baking soda, salt, and flour. Gradually add the dry ingredients to the banana mixture and stir until just combined.
4. Fold in the chopped walnuts.
5. Pour the batter into the prepared loaf pan and bake for 60-65 minutes, or until a toothpick inserted into the center comes out clean.
6. Let cool in the pan for 10 minutes, then transfer to a wire rack to cool completely.

Peach Galette

Ingredients:

- **For the crust:**
    - 1 1/2 cups all-purpose flour
    - 2 tbsp granulated sugar
    - 1/2 tsp salt
    - 1/2 cup unsalted butter, cold and cubed
    - 4-5 tbsp ice water
- **For the filling:**
    - 4-5 ripe peaches, sliced
    - 2 tbsp granulated sugar
    - 1 tbsp cornstarch
    - 1/2 tsp cinnamon
    - 1 tbsp lemon juice
- **For brushing:**
    - 1 tbsp heavy cream
    - 1 tbsp turbinado sugar

Instructions:

1. **For the crust:** In a food processor, pulse together the flour, sugar, and salt. Add the cold butter and pulse until the mixture resembles coarse crumbs. Gradually add the ice water, pulsing until the dough comes together. Shape the dough into a disk, wrap in plastic, and refrigerate for at least 1 hour.
2. **For the filling:** In a bowl, combine the peaches, sugar, cornstarch, cinnamon, and lemon juice.
3. Preheat the oven to 375°F (190°C) and line a baking sheet with parchment paper.
4. Roll out the dough on a floured surface into a 12-inch circle. Transfer to the prepared baking sheet. Spoon the peach mixture onto the center, leaving a border. Fold the edges of the dough over the filling, pleating as you go.
5. Brush the edges of the dough with heavy cream and sprinkle with turbinado sugar.
6. Bake for 40-45 minutes, until the crust is golden and the filling is bubbling. Let cool before serving.

Tiramisu

Ingredients:

- 1 1/2 cups brewed espresso, cooled
- 1/4 cup coffee liqueur (optional)
- 1 1/2 cups mascarpone cheese
- 1 1/4 cups heavy cream
- 1/2 cup granulated sugar
- 1 tsp vanilla extract
- 2 large egg yolks
- 1 package ladyfinger cookies (savoiardi)
- Unsweetened cocoa powder, for dusting

Instructions:

1. In a shallow dish, combine the espresso and coffee liqueur. Set aside.
2. In a large bowl, whisk together the mascarpone, heavy cream, sugar, vanilla, and egg yolks until smooth and fluffy.
3. Briefly dip the ladyfingers into the espresso mixture (do not soak them). Arrange a layer of dipped ladyfingers at the bottom of a 9x13-inch dish.
4. Spread half of the mascarpone mixture over the ladyfingers. Repeat with another layer of dipped ladyfingers and the remaining mascarpone mixture.
5. Cover and refrigerate for at least 4 hours, preferably overnight.
6. Before serving, dust with cocoa powder and enjoy!

Zucchini Bread

Ingredients:

- 2 cups all-purpose flour
- 1 tsp baking soda
- 1/2 tsp baking powder
- 1/2 tsp salt
- 1 tsp cinnamon
- 1/2 tsp nutmeg
- 1/2 cup granulated sugar
- 1/2 cup brown sugar, packed
- 2 large eggs
- 1 tsp vanilla extract
- 1 1/2 cups shredded zucchini (about 1 medium zucchini)
- 1/2 cup vegetable oil
- 1/2 cup chopped walnuts (optional)

Instructions:

1. Preheat the oven to 350°F (175°C) and grease a loaf pan.
2. In a large bowl, whisk together the flour, baking soda, baking powder, salt, cinnamon, and nutmeg.
3. In another bowl, beat together the sugars, eggs, and vanilla extract. Stir in the shredded zucchini and oil.
4. Gradually add the dry ingredients to the wet ingredients, mixing until just combined. Fold in the walnuts (if using).
5. Pour the batter into the prepared loaf pan and bake for 55-60 minutes, or until a toothpick inserted into the center comes out clean.
6. Let cool in the pan for 10 minutes before transferring to a wire rack to cool completely.

Classic Cheesecake

Ingredients:

- **For the crust:**
    - 1 1/2 cups graham cracker crumbs
    - 1/4 cup granulated sugar
    - 1/2 cup unsalted butter, melted
- **For the filling:**
    - 3 packages (8 oz each) cream cheese, softened
    - 1 cup granulated sugar
    - 3 large eggs
    - 1 tsp vanilla extract
    - 1/2 cup sour cream

Instructions:

1. Preheat the oven to 325°F (165°C) and grease a 9-inch springform pan.
2. **For the crust:** In a bowl, combine the graham cracker crumbs, sugar, and melted butter. Press the mixture into the bottom of the pan. Bake for 10 minutes, then let cool.
3. **For the filling:** Beat the cream cheese and sugar until smooth. Add the eggs, one at a time, mixing well after each addition. Stir in the vanilla extract and sour cream.
4. Pour the filling into the cooled crust and bake for 50-60 minutes, or until the edges are set but the center is slightly jiggly.
5. Let cool completely before refrigerating for at least 4 hours or overnight.
6. Serve plain or topped with fresh berries.

Raspberry Almond Bars

Ingredients:

- 1 cup all-purpose flour
- 1/2 cup almond flour
- 1/2 tsp baking powder
- 1/4 tsp salt
- 1/2 cup unsalted butter, softened
- 1/2 cup granulated sugar
- 1 large egg
- 1 tsp vanilla extract
- 1/4 cup raspberry jam
- Sliced almonds, for topping

Instructions:

1. Preheat the oven to 350°F (175°C) and line an 8x8-inch baking pan with parchment paper.
2. In a bowl, whisk together the flour, almond flour, baking powder, and salt.
3. In a separate bowl, beat the butter and sugar until light and fluffy. Add the egg and vanilla extract and mix well.
4. Gradually add the dry ingredients to the butter mixture and mix until just combined.
5. Press the dough into the prepared pan and spread the raspberry jam evenly over the top. Sprinkle with sliced almonds.
6. Bake for 25-30 minutes, or until golden brown. Let cool before cutting into bars.

Apricot Danish

Ingredients:

- 1 sheet puff pastry, thawed
- 1/2 cup apricot preserves
- 4 oz cream cheese, softened
- 1 tbsp powdered sugar
- 1 tsp vanilla extract
- 1 egg (for egg wash)

Instructions:

1. Preheat the oven to 400°F (200°C) and line a baking sheet with parchment paper.
2. Roll out the puff pastry on a floured surface and cut into 4 squares.
3. In a small bowl, mix together the cream cheese, powdered sugar, and vanilla extract.
4. Spread a tablespoon of cream cheese mixture onto the center of each puff pastry square.
5. Spoon a tablespoon of apricot preserves on top of the cream cheese.
6. Fold the corners of the puff pastry towards the center to form a pocket.
7. Brush with egg wash (beaten egg) and bake for 15-20 minutes, or until golden brown.
8. Let cool before serving.

Cardamom Bread

Ingredients:

- 3 cups all-purpose flour
- 1 packet active dry yeast (2 1/4 tsp)
- 1/4 cup sugar
- 1 tsp ground cardamom
- 1/2 tsp salt
- 1/2 cup warm milk (about 110°F)
- 1/4 cup unsalted butter, melted
- 2 large eggs
- 1/2 cup chopped pistachios or almonds (optional)
- 1/4 cup honey (for glazing)

Instructions:

1. In a large bowl, mix the flour, yeast, sugar, cardamom, and salt.
2. In a separate bowl, whisk together the warm milk, melted butter, and eggs. Add this mixture to the dry ingredients and stir to form a dough.
3. Knead the dough on a floured surface for about 10 minutes, until smooth. Add chopped nuts if desired.
4. Place the dough in a greased bowl, cover with a cloth, and let rise for 1-1.5 hours, or until doubled in size.
5. Preheat the oven to 350°F (175°C). Punch down the dough and shape it into a loaf or braid.
6. Place the dough on a greased baking sheet and bake for 25-30 minutes, or until golden brown.
7. Brush with warm honey and let cool before slicing.

Fig and Walnut Bread

Ingredients:

- 2 cups whole wheat flour
- 1 cup all-purpose flour
- 1 1/2 tsp baking powder
- 1/2 tsp salt
- 1 tsp ground cinnamon
- 1/2 cup unsalted butter, softened
- 1/2 cup brown sugar
- 2 eggs
- 1 cup dried figs, chopped
- 1/2 cup chopped walnuts
- 1 tsp vanilla extract
- 1/2 cup buttermilk

Instructions:

1. Preheat the oven to 350°F (175°C) and grease a loaf pan.
2. In a bowl, whisk together the whole wheat flour, all-purpose flour, baking powder, salt, and cinnamon.
3. In another bowl, cream the butter and brown sugar until light and fluffy. Add the eggs, one at a time, beating well after each addition. Stir in the vanilla extract.
4. Gradually add the dry ingredients to the wet mixture, alternating with buttermilk. Fold in the chopped figs and walnuts.
5. Pour the batter into the prepared loaf pan and bake for 50-55 minutes, or until a toothpick inserted into the center comes out clean.
6. Allow the bread to cool in the pan for 10 minutes before transferring to a wire rack to cool completely.

Key Lime Pie

Ingredients:

- **For the crust:**
    - 1 1/2 cups graham cracker crumbs
    - 1/4 cup granulated sugar
    - 1/2 cup unsalted butter, melted
- **For the filling:**
    - 1 can (14 oz) sweetened condensed milk
    - 1/2 cup key lime juice (fresh or bottled)
    - 4 large egg yolks
- **For the topping:**
    - 1 cup heavy cream
    - 2 tbsp powdered sugar
    - 1 tsp vanilla extract

Instructions:

1. **For the crust:** Preheat the oven to 350°F (175°C). In a bowl, combine the graham cracker crumbs, sugar, and melted butter. Press the mixture into the bottom of a pie dish to form an even crust. Bake for 8-10 minutes, then let cool.
2. **For the filling:** In a bowl, whisk together the sweetened condensed milk, key lime juice, and egg yolks until smooth. Pour the filling into the cooled crust.
3. Bake for 15-20 minutes, or until the filling is set and slightly firm.
4. Let cool to room temperature, then refrigerate for at least 4 hours or overnight.
5. **For the topping:** In a chilled bowl, whip the heavy cream, powdered sugar, and vanilla extract until stiff peaks form. Spread the whipped cream on top of the pie before serving.

Pumpkin Spice Cake

Ingredients:

- 2 cups all-purpose flour
- 1 1/2 tsp baking soda
- 1 1/2 tsp ground cinnamon
- 1/2 tsp ground nutmeg
- 1/2 tsp ground ginger
- 1/4 tsp salt
- 1/2 cup unsalted butter, softened
- 1 cup granulated sugar
- 1 cup pumpkin puree
- 2 large eggs
- 1 tsp vanilla extract
- 1/2 cup buttermilk

Instructions:

1. Preheat the oven to 350°F (175°C) and grease two 9-inch round cake pans.
2. In a bowl, whisk together the flour, baking soda, cinnamon, nutmeg, ginger, and salt.
3. In a separate bowl, beat the butter and sugar until light and fluffy. Add the pumpkin puree, eggs, and vanilla extract, mixing well.
4. Gradually add the dry ingredients to the wet mixture, alternating with the buttermilk.
5. Divide the batter between the two prepared cake pans and bake for 30-35 minutes, or until a toothpick inserted into the center comes out clean.
6. Allow the cakes to cool in the pans for 10 minutes, then transfer to a wire rack to cool completely before frosting.

Chocolate Hazelnut Tart

Ingredients:

- **For the crust:**
    - 1 1/4 cups all-purpose flour
    - 1/4 cup cocoa powder
    - 1/4 cup granulated sugar
    - 1/2 cup unsalted butter, cold and cubed
    - 1 large egg yolk
    - 2 tbsp cold water
- **For the filling:**
    - 1/2 cup heavy cream
    - 1 cup dark chocolate, chopped
    - 1/4 cup sugar
    - 1/4 cup hazelnut spread (like Nutella)
    - 1/4 cup chopped toasted hazelnuts

Instructions:

1. **For the crust:** Preheat the oven to 350°F (175°C). In a food processor, combine the flour, cocoa powder, and sugar. Add the cold butter and pulse until the mixture resembles coarse crumbs. Add the egg yolk and cold water, and pulse until the dough comes together. Press the dough into the bottom of a tart pan and bake for 10-12 minutes. Let cool.
2. **For the filling:** In a saucepan, heat the heavy cream until it begins to simmer. Pour the cream over the chopped chocolate and let sit for 5 minutes. Stir until smooth, then mix in the hazelnut spread.
3. Pour the filling into the cooled tart crust and refrigerate for at least 2 hours or until set.
4. Once set, sprinkle with chopped hazelnuts before serving.

Pear and Almond Cake

Ingredients:

- 2 large ripe pears, peeled and sliced
- 1 cup all-purpose flour
- 1/2 cup almond flour
- 1 tsp baking powder
- 1/4 tsp salt
- 1/2 cup unsalted butter, softened
- 3/4 cup granulated sugar
- 2 large eggs
- 1 tsp vanilla extract
- 1/4 cup milk
- 1/4 cup sliced almonds (for topping)
- Powdered sugar for dusting

Instructions:

1. Preheat the oven to 350°F (175°C) and grease a 9-inch round cake pan.
2. In a bowl, whisk together the all-purpose flour, almond flour, baking powder, and salt.
3. In another bowl, cream the butter and sugar together until light and fluffy. Add the eggs one at a time, beating well after each addition. Stir in the vanilla extract.
4. Gradually add the dry ingredients to the wet mixture, alternating with the milk, and mix until smooth.
5. Pour the batter into the prepared cake pan and gently arrange the pear slices on top.
6. Sprinkle the sliced almonds over the top and bake for 35-40 minutes, or until a toothpick inserted into the center comes out clean.
7. Let the cake cool in the pan for 10 minutes before transferring to a wire rack. Dust with powdered sugar before serving.

Nutella Swirl Bread

Ingredients:

- 3 cups all-purpose flour
- 1 packet active dry yeast (2 1/4 tsp)
- 1/4 cup granulated sugar
- 1/2 tsp salt
- 1 cup warm milk (110°F)
- 1/4 cup unsalted butter, melted
- 2 large eggs
- 1/2 cup Nutella (chocolate-hazelnut spread)

Instructions:

1. In a large bowl, combine the flour, yeast, sugar, and salt.
2. In a separate bowl, whisk together the warm milk, melted butter, and eggs. Add the wet ingredients to the dry ingredients and stir to form a dough.
3. Knead the dough on a floured surface for about 10 minutes, until smooth. Place in a greased bowl, cover with a cloth, and let rise for 1 hour or until doubled in size.
4. Punch down the dough and roll it out into a rectangle. Spread Nutella evenly over the dough.
5. Roll the dough tightly into a log and place it in a greased loaf pan. Let rise for another 30 minutes.
6. Preheat the oven to 350°F (175°C) and bake for 25-30 minutes, or until golden brown. Let cool before slicing.

Honey and Lavender Madeleines

Ingredients:

- 1 cup all-purpose flour
- 1/2 tsp baking powder
- 1/4 tsp salt
- 1/4 cup unsalted butter, melted
- 2 large eggs
- 1/2 cup granulated sugar
- 2 tbsp honey
- 1 tsp dried lavender buds
- 1 tsp vanilla extract

Instructions:

1. Preheat the oven to 375°F (190°C) and grease a madeleine pan.
2. In a bowl, whisk together the flour, baking powder, and salt.
3. In another bowl, beat the eggs and sugar together until pale and fluffy. Stir in the honey, melted butter, vanilla extract, and lavender.
4. Gradually fold in the dry ingredients until just combined.
5. Spoon the batter into the madeleine pan, filling each mold about 2/3 full.
6. Bake for 10-12 minutes, or until the madeleines are golden brown and spring back when touched.
7. Let cool in the pan for a few minutes before transferring to a wire rack. Serve dusted with powdered sugar if desired.

Salted Caramel Brownies

Ingredients:

- **For the brownies:**
    - 1 cup unsalted butter, melted
    - 1 1/4 cups granulated sugar
    - 1/2 cup unsweetened cocoa powder
    - 3 large eggs
    - 1 tsp vanilla extract
    - 1 cup all-purpose flour
    - 1/2 tsp salt
- **For the salted caramel sauce:**
    - 1/2 cup unsalted butter
    - 1 cup brown sugar
    - 1/2 cup heavy cream
    - 1 tsp vanilla extract
    - 1 tsp sea salt

Instructions:

1. **For the brownies:** Preheat the oven to 350°F (175°C) and grease an 8x8-inch baking pan.
2. In a bowl, mix the melted butter, sugar, and cocoa powder. Add the eggs and vanilla extract and beat until smooth. Stir in the flour and salt.
3. Pour the brownie batter into the prepared pan and bake for 20-25 minutes, or until a toothpick inserted comes out with a few moist crumbs. Let the brownies cool in the pan.
4. **For the caramel sauce:** In a saucepan, melt the butter over medium heat. Stir in the brown sugar and heavy cream, then bring to a simmer. Cook for 3-5 minutes, stirring constantly, until the sauce thickens.
5. Remove from heat and stir in the vanilla extract and sea salt.
6. Pour the salted caramel sauce over the cooled brownies. Let set for 10 minutes before slicing and serving.

Sweet Potato Pie

Ingredients:

- 1 lb sweet potatoes, peeled and cubed
- 1/2 cup unsalted butter, softened
- 1 cup brown sugar
- 2 large eggs
- 1/2 tsp cinnamon
- 1/4 tsp nutmeg
- 1/4 tsp ground ginger
- 1/2 tsp vanilla extract
- 1/2 cup heavy cream
- 1 pre-baked pie crust (9-inch)

Instructions:

1. Preheat the oven to 350°F (175°C).
2. Boil the sweet potatoes in a large pot until tender, about 15-20 minutes. Drain and mash them until smooth.
3. In a large bowl, combine the mashed sweet potatoes, butter, brown sugar, eggs, spices, vanilla extract, and heavy cream. Mix until smooth.
4. Pour the filling into the pre-baked pie crust and smooth the top.
5. Bake for 45-50 minutes, or until the filling is set and a knife inserted into the center comes out clean.
6. Allow the pie to cool before serving. Top with whipped cream if desired.